Road Trip: Exploring America's Regions

LET'S EXPLORE THE

SOUTHWEST

BY KATHLEEN CONNORS

Gareth Stevens
Publishing

Please visit our website, www.garethstevens.com. For a free color catalog of all our high-quality books, call toll free 1-800-542-2595 or fax 1-877-542-2596.

Library of Congress Cataloging-in-Publication Data

Connors, Kathleen.
Let's explore the Southwest / Kathleen Connors.
    pages cm. — (Road trip : exploring America's regions)
Includes index.
ISBN 978-1-4339-9150-9 (pbk.)
ISBN 978-1-4339-9151-6 (6-pack)
ISBN 978-1-4339-9149-3 (library binding)
1. Southwest, New—Juvenile literature. 2. Texas—Juvenile literature. I. Title.
F786.C76 2014
979—dc23

2013000101

First Edition

Published in 2014 by
Gareth Stevens Publishing
111 East 14th Street, Suite 349
New York, NY 10003

Copyright © 2014 Gareth Stevens Publishing

Designer: Andrea Davison-Bartolotta
Editor: Kristen Rajczak

Photo credits: Cover, pp. 1 (both), 4, 5 (map, background), 8, 11, 14, 15 (yellow note) 21 iStockphoto/Thinkstock; cover, back cover, interior backgrounds (texture) Marilyn Volan/Shutterstock.com; cover, back cover (map) Stacey Lynne Payne/Shutterstock.com; cover, back cover, pp. 1, 3, 22–24 (green sign) Shutterstock.com; interior backgrounds (road) Renata Novackova/Shutterstock.com, (blue sign) Vitezslav Valka/Shutterstock.com; p. 5 (curled corner) JonnyDrake/Shutterstock.com; p. 6 M.Ellinger/Shutterstock.com; p. 7 sursad/Shutterstock.com; p. 9 Pete McBride/National Geographic/Getty Images; p. 10 Ernestro Burciaga/The Image Bank/Getty Images; p. 13 Richard Cummins/Lonely Planet Images/Getty Images; p. 15 (top) Melissa Brandes/Shutterstock.com, (bottom) Ffooter/Shutterstock.com; p. 16 Ysbrand Cosijn/Shutterstock.com; p. 17 (main) Rob Wilson/Shutterstock.com, (inset) Andrew Zarivny/Shutterstock.com; p. 19 (main) Timothy Riese/Shutterstock.com, (inset) nito/Shutterstock.com; p. 20 Jason Merritt/Getty Images.

Printed in the United States of America

CPSIA compliance information: Batch #CS13GS: For further information contact Gareth Stevens, New York, New York at 1-800-542-2595.

Contents

Words in the glossary appear in **bold** type the first time they are used in the text.

Check Out the Southwest!

Though old movies often show the Southwest as a bare landscape full of cowboys, there's lots to see in this part of the United States! From the towering Rocky Mountains to the lights of Los Angeles, California, the Southwest is full of **destinations** for every traveler!

The states of New Mexico, Arizona, Utah, and southern Colorado make up the Southwest. Southern California, Nevada, Texas, and Oklahoma will be included here, too, since they share some history and **culture** with these states.

The Southwest

Pit Stop

In general, the Southwest has **arid** weather. A large part of it is desert, and many areas of the **region** don't have much rain.

4

Some states are included in more than one US region. Texas and Oklahoma are often called part of the South. California is often called the West Coast, though Northern California can be considered part of the Pacific Northwest, too.

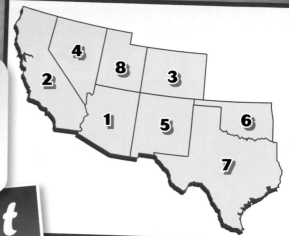

The Southwest
at a Glance

	State	Population (2010)	Date of Statehood	Capital	State Bird	State Flower
1	Arizona	6,392,017	Feb. 14, 1912	Phoenix	cactus wren	saguaro cactus flower
2	California	37,253,956	Sept. 9, 1850	Sacramento	California valley quail	California poppy
3	Colorado	5,029,196	Aug. 1, 1876	Denver	lark bunting	columbine
4	Nevada	2,700,551	Oct. 31, 1864	Carson City	mountain bluebird	sagebrush
5	New Mexico	2,059,179	Jan. 6, 1912	Santa Fe	roadrunner	yucca flower
6	Oklahoma	3,751,351	Nov. 16, 1907	Oklahoma City	scissor-tailed flycatcher	mistletoe
7	Texas	25,145,561	Dec. 29, 1845	Austin	northern mockingbird	bluebonnet
8	Utah	2,763,885	Jan. 4, 1896	Salt Lake City	California seagull	sego lily

The Lay of the Land

The grand Rocky Mountains are worth a road trip to the Southwest! They're one of the main features of the region, particularly in New Mexico and Colorado. The Colorado Plateau offers extraordinary scenery, too. The red-colored rocks of its cliffs and canyons are popular with hikers and climbers.

Though dry, the Southwest has several national forests and a national grassland within its states. Petrified Forest National Park in northeastern Arizona has many trees that have been petrified, which means they've turned to stone!

Pit Stop

The most famous geographic feature of the Southwest—and perhaps even the whole United States—is the Grand Canyon. Some people hike through all 277 miles (446 km) of it!

The Southern Rockies have some of the highest peaks in the whole Rocky Mountain range, which is found from the Southwest all the way into Canada.

Big Rivers

The Southwest has two major rivers. The Colorado River flows through Colorado, Utah, New Mexico, Nevada, Arizona, and California. The Rio Grande divides Texas and Mexico.

The Rio Grande flows into the Gulf of Mexico, the body of water on the southeast border of Texas. In southwest Texas, you can visit Big Bend National Park, named after a bend in the Rio Grande. There are 150 miles (241 km) of trails to hike there. In fact, it's the largest area without roads in the state!

Pit Stop

Have you ever been in two places at once? At the Four Corners, you can be in four! There, the state lines of New Mexico, Arizona, Colorado, and Utah meet.

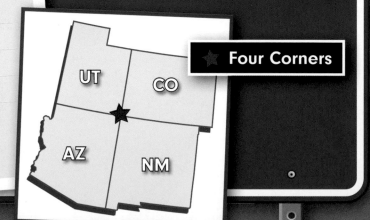

⭐ Four Corners

UT

CO

AZ

NM

The Colorado River flows through the Grand Canyon. Many people take rafting trips on this big river.

Southwestern Tribes

The history of the Southwest is tightly tied to Native American tribes in the region. Some of the largest tribes include the Pueblo, Navajo, and Apache. Today, more than 20 percent of Native Americans in the United States live in this region.

The Navajo have lived in the Southwest between 800 and 1,000 years. The Navajo Nation **Reservation** found near the Four Corners is the largest reservation in the country. It's about the size of West Virginia!

Pit Stop

At the Navajo National Monument in Navajo, Arizona, visitors can explore cliff homes of ancient Pueblos. They date back more than 750 years!

Zuni Pueblo dancers

The Pueblo tribes living in the Southwest are **descendants** of the Ancestral Pueblo Culture who settled in the region hundreds of years ago. You can see homes and villages they built!

11

The Start of Settlement

The Spanish explored the Southwest during the late 1500s. They lived side by side with the Native American tribes in the region and were the only Europeans in the Southwest for more than 200 years. By the 1800s, much of the Southwest was owned by Mexico.

It's common today to hear Spanish spoken in the Southwest region, especially the closer to the Mexican border you travel. Knowing a few simple words and phrases could help you ask for directions on a road trip!

Pit Stop

Many places in the Southwest have Spanish names, such Santa Fe, the capital city of New Mexico. The Spanish founded Santa Fe in 1610.

Many of the Spanish settlements in the Southwest began as missions. Missions were centers of the Christian faith.

13

Southwest Culture

The Southwest's Spanish **heritage** and rich Native American history have greatly affected its culture. Buildings and homes in southwestern cities are often modeled after the Pueblo tribes' **adobe** style. Art from this region commonly features Native American stories and ideas.

Southwestern **cuisine** borrows largely from the combined cultures of its past. One of the most popular food styles is Tex-Mex. Tex-Mex combines Mexican cuisine with the more American tastes of Texas and the Southwest. Tex-Mex meals commonly include tacos, burritos, beans, and fresh salsas.

adobe-style home

Southwestern Salsa

Ingredients:

1 can black beans, drained
2 8-ounce cans corn, not drained
1/2 orange, red, or yellow bell pepper, chopped
1/2 purple onion, diced
2–3 jalapeño peppers (optional to remove seeds)
4 large tomatoes, diced
1 tbsp olive oil
1/2 tsp salt
1 tsp cumin
1/4 cup cilantro, chopped and firmly packed
the juice of 3 limes

Directions:

Mix all the ingredients together. Serve with your favorite chips or on tacos!

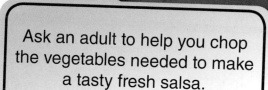

Ask an adult to help you chop the vegetables needed to make a tasty fresh salsa.

Pit Stop

Downtown Santa Fe, New Mexico, has 400-year-old adobe buildings, such as the Palace of the Governors. The Palace was built in the early 17th century and is still in use today as a historical museum.

Palace of the Governors

Texas

Even in its name, the state of Texas is **influenced** by Spanish and Native American culture. Texas is a Spanish name, but it comes from the Native American word for "friends" or "allies."

Texas is full of exciting places to visit on a road trip. San Antonio is the second most populous city in Texas with more than 1.3 million people. It's also one of the most visited places in Texas as the location of the Alamo. In 1836, Texas was fighting for independence from Mexico, and this old Spanish mission was the site of an important battle.

Visitors to the Alamo learn about the many parts the building has played in Texas history.

Pit Stop

Post

Houston, we have a problem! Have you ever heard this line in a movie about space? That's because NASA's Mission Control Center is at the Lyndon B. Johnson Space Center in Texas's largest city—Houston.

Houston skyline

The City of Angels

The second-largest city in the United States draws many **tourists** to the Southwest—Los Angeles, California! With a population of about 3.8 million, Los Angeles is home to TV and movie studios that you can visit. Sports fans can catch a Dodgers baseball game, the Clippers shooting hoops, or the Kings during hockey season.

Another large southwestern city—Phoenix, Arizona—has a population of about 1.4 million. Many people like to visit Phoenix since it's one of the sunniest places in the country!

Pit Stop

One of the most famous places in the Southwest isn't a big city. Roswell, New Mexico, is known as the location of a UFO (unidentified flying object) crash in 1947. Some say there were **extraterrestrials** on the UFO!

Sometimes people call Los Angeles "Hollywood," but Hollywood is just one part of the huge city!

Born or Raised

From presidents to athletes, many familiar faces were born in the Southwest. Both President Dwight D. Eisenhower and President Lyndon B. Johnson were born in Texas. Lady Bird Johnson, President Johnson's wife and the First Lady, also hailed from this big state.

Country singers Carrie Underwood and Garth Brooks are both Oklahoma natives. So is basketball star Blake Griffin! Baseball great Mickey Mantle was born in Oklahoma, too. The old barn Mantle used to practice in still stands in Commerce, Oklahoma.

Carrie Underwood

Weird and Wonderful Pit Stops in the Southwest

Rooster Cogburn Ostrich Ranch
Phoenix, Arizona
Take a tour of this large ostrich ranch in a monster truck. You can even feed an ostrich!

World's Largest Pop Bottle
Arcadia, Oklahoma
See a huge, light-up pop bottle along Route 66 and get a cold drink from the connected store.

International UFO Center
Roswell, New Mexico
Visit a museum all about the UFO that's said to have crashed near Roswell in 1947.

Cadillac Ranch
Amarillo, Texas
Bring a can of spray paint to leave your mark on the 10 Cadillacs half-buried near Amarillo.

Glossary

adobe: built out of bricks made of clay or earth dried in the sun

arid: dry

cuisine: a style of cooking

culture: the beliefs and ways of life of a group of people

descendant: a person who comes after another in a family

destination: the place someone is traveling to

extraterrestrial: a being not from Earth

heritage: something that comes from past members of a family or group

influence: to have an effect on

region: an area

reservation: a piece of land set aside for a group of people, such as Native Americans

tourist: a person traveling to visit a place

For More Information

Books

McDaniel, Melissa. *Southwest Indians.* Chicago, IL: Heinemann Library, 2012.

Orr, Tamra. *It's Cool to Learn About the United States. Southwest.* Ann Arbor, MI: Cherry Lake Publishing, 2012.

Rau, Dana Meachen. *The Southwest.* New York, NY: Children's Press, 2012.

Websites

Best of the Southwest
adventure.nationalgeographic.com/adventure/trips/southwest-united-states/
Read more about the Southwest region as well as see awesome photos and maps.

States and Regions
www.harcourtschool.com/ss1/adventure_activities/grade4.html
Use this interactive website to learn more about the regions of the United States.

Index